Voices Of The Valley

A love note for my home Kashmir.

Dr. Upasana Kachroo

BookLeaf Publishing

India | USA | UK

Made with ❤ on the BookLeaf Publishing Platform

www.bookleafpub.in

www.bookleafpub.com

Dedication

To our beloved parents,

Who gifted us the treasure of childhood in the
paradise that is Kashmir,

Whose stories and memories are the threads that
weave through these verses,

For the laughter, the lessons, and the love that
filled our days with light,

And for nurturing in us a deep-rooted
appreciation for a homeland that lives forever in
our hearts.

This book is a tribute to your enduring strength,
your unwavering hope, and the profound beauty
you instilled in our souls.

With all our love,

Karuna & Neetu

Acknowledgement

This book would not have been possible without the love, guidance, and inspiration of those who have shaped my life and nourished my soul.

First and foremost, I want to express my heartfelt gratitude to my parents, who taught me to love above all else. Your unwavering care and wisdom have been the bedrock of my life, and your lessons on resilience have permeated every word of this book.

To my elder sister, Karuna Didi, who embodies innocence and purity. Your presence in my life has been a source of endless joy and comfort. I also thank you for giving me the sweetest, most lovable nephew in the world. I love you, Saiyyam.

My deepest appreciation goes to my grandparents, with a special mention to my Baipyarajee, who first introduced me to the nuances of poetry. Your passion for literature was infectious, and it is because of you that I found my voice in words.

To my husband, Arvind, who is a calm sea of serenity and warmth. The easy silence you create for me, has always been my anchor.

To my children, Sai and Arya, who inspire me every day to be a better mother and person. You are the light of my life and the reason I strive to share our stories and keep the legacy of Kashmir alive.

And finally, my deepest gratitude to the very air, soil, and water of the valley—the essence of Kashmir that flows through my veins. You are my muse, my connection to a land that lives on in every breath I take.

Thank you to everyone who has been a part of this journey. This book is as much yours as it is mine...

Preface

This book is a journey back to a time and place that shaped my very being—a place where the air was filled with the scent of chinar leaves, where the mountains stood tall and majestic, where the brooks sang their timeless songs, and where life was as simple as it was profound. It is a collection of memories, not just mine, but of all the Kashmiri Pandits who once called this paradise home.

These poems are for those who never had the chance to play in the snow of their motherland, to feel the cool breeze of the valley, or to hear the stories passed down through generations by the warmth of a kangri.

To those who know little of our life in the valley, I offer these verses as a window into a world that was lost to us, but never forgotten. Kashmir continues to live in our hearts and in the stories we pass on to our children.

May these poems serve as a bridge between the past and the present, and as a testament to the beauty, the resilience, and the spirit of the valley and its people.

Contents

Hameen Asto

If there is a paradise on earth,
It is here, it is here, it is here.
Where fragrant flowers in wild hues sway,
And shepherds lead their flocks at break of day.
Oh, tender fields where my young heart played,
Feeding sheep beneath the chinar's shade.
In our garden, a realm of colours strewn,
Both sisters danced and let our bodies swoon.
We chased the butterflies through scented air,
While lush fields sighed and whispered their
prayer.
The sun, like a blessing, crowned our heads,
As we hopped and skipped in the flowerbeds.

To the lake we would wander, my grandparents and I,
Nodding and waving, such smiles O my!
The water, a mirror to the heavens above,
Reflecting the beauty of all we loved.
In Raghunath mandir, we'd kneel in prayer,
The flame of devotion flickering there.
And for the grand fests, to Tulmul we'd go,
Or climb to Shankaracharya, with fervour albeit slow.
This, my home, my world, my all,
Has streams and brooks that speak with a deep drawl.
In the arms of the mountain, where beauty still reigns,
And boundless joy flows free in the valley's veins.
So, if there is a paradise on earth,
It is here, it is here, it is here.
In the laughter of children, in the song of the breeze,
In the dance of the flowers, and in the whispering trees.

Hukkus Bukkus, Who Are We?

Hukkus Bukkus, who are we?
Tell us now, what is the key?
In this garden where the colours sway,
We wile away time, its endless play.
Who are you and who am I?
And who is it that dwells nearby,
The one who lives in all we see,
Binding us for eternity?
Laughter rings, we break into song
Through the mud, where our shoeless feet belong.
"Who am I, and who are you?"
Through this game, we seek what's true.
Onum Battoukh, the feast is grand,
But ties me down with a gentle hand.

Like the rice in its pot, we're bound,
Worldly ways tie us to the ground.
Shwaas Kichh Kichh, with every breath we take,
Our souls are cleansed of every mistake.
A serenity flows as the sparrows sing,
We listen close to the melodies they bring.
Bhruman Daras, bathed in pure light,
when I touch that truth so bright,
Our elders watch on, with knowing eyes,
As we dance beneath deific skies.
Teykis Tyakkha, the children so bold,
Mark of saffron, between their brows.
Their spirits akin to a sandalwood tree,
Already fragrant with divinity.
Hukkus Bukkus, who are we?
Children of the valley, wild and free.

Winter's Embrace

O snow, thou tender veil of night,
Descend in silence, soft and slight.
Thy alabaster touch, so cold and still,
Wraps the valley in a dreamlike chill.
In thee, O snow, a tranquil world appears,
Where mountains stand as ancient seers,
Guardians of our winter's rite,
In thy quietude, we find respite.
Thou art the breath of frost's sweet kiss,
The harbinger of a season's bliss.
As thou dost fall, so soft and slow,
Thou bid'st us gather 'round the glow.
Beneath the layf's woven fold,
We seek thy warmth, though thou art cold.

Kangri's fire, a gentle burn,
In thy frigid arms, we to thee return.
Thou art the keeper of the hush profound,
Wherein our souls in quiet found,
A refuge from the perpetual din,
Of life's cruel race, of loss and sin.
O snow, thou art the hand of fate,
That doth our fragile bonds create.
In thee, we find a sacred peace,
Where stories shared do never cease.
Thy crystals fall, a myriad bright,
Each one a star in winter's night.
They speak of lands both lost and found,
Of memories that in thee are bound.
So, fall O snow, in gentle dance,
Enrobe the earth in thy romance.
For in thy beauty, cold and pure,
Our hearts are warm, our love is sure.
And when the thaw of spring appears,
To melt away our sorry fears,
We'll carry forth thy tender grace,
A memory of thy soft embrace.

The Nocturne Of Herath

Upon the valley's shuddering breath, Herath
descends,
Pouring itself into our homes, while the moonlight
slowly bends,
The night into a festival of shadows, where the
sacred and the still,
Dance and then converge beneath the Zabarwan's
tranquil hill.
Clay vessels gleam, kissed by the river's ancient
flow,
Gurgles of water follow the devotees into fields
below

They whisper of Shiva smeared in ash, sitting in
silence profound,
As his loyal clan prepares for the betrothal, with a
joy newfound.
The kangri cradles an amber warmth in its woven
embrace,
While wonderous tales are told of a special time
and place,
Kailash, they call it, where mountains wore, crowns
of crystal snow,
And rivers sang secrets of yore, as they splashed
and flowed.
With hearts full and eyes that gleam with salty
waters of joy,
All worship the One, Mahadev, who now seems
suddenly coy.
At the prospect of leaving his tiger skin and prized
trident behind,
And decked in a blazing glow, forced to step out of
his shrine.
As the cosmos comes together to celebrate this
celestial affair,
Sages chant and families bow, in awe of this
heavenly pair,
The night unfurls, as sleepy eyes cling to a
cherished hymn,
Lost in prayer, just barely awake, as the dark
leisurely dims.

Shivratri slowly concludes, as the break of morn
draws near,
We offer flowers, unbeaten rice, and sugar columns
clear.
To the Kalash, where holy waters swell, with
hopeful hands we pour,
In reverence, our humble gifts, as the call of conch
soars.
The prayer's final echo drifts, as the sacred fire
wanes,
Its fumes swirl tenderly, into the day that yet
remains.
The next light bears witness, to fresh prayers
whispered low,
The embers twinkle, fed with faith anew, in a quiet
steady glow.
Walnuts slumber, in the water's grasp,
Cracked by dawn's tender clasp.
Revealing within their hardened shell,
A holy offering, where blessings dwell.
The prasad earned is a tchot of rice and the
walnuts steeped overnight,
Shared with all, this humble feast brings fasting
bellies some respite.
And as the sacred day unfolds, the young with glee
receive,
Herath Kharch in hands outstretched, a gift on this
festive eve.

Salaam, they call it, the day of joy, where union
divine, we hail,
Celebrations are the order of the day, as hearts and
spirits sail.
Revel in this festival of love and faith, beneath the
Zabarwan's reach,
'Cause Herath's hallowed history teaches lessons of
true peace.

An Embroidered Tale

The wind was a whisper through Srinagar's streets,
As mother and daughter strode,
Through alleys where merchants with calls so
sweet,
Ushered them into their abode.
The child, with a frown, her interest worn thin,
Followed her mother's guiding hand,
Not knowing the treasures that lay within
The folds of the market's stand.
"Must we buy woollens, dreary and old?"
She murmured in a voice so blue,
But the mother, with secrets yet untold,
Led on, as if without a clue.

The shawls were unrolled, with a flourish and fan,
Sozni in its elegance gleamed bright,
As the evening dimmed, and shadows ran,
Each stitch a dance of light.
The daughter's eyes, once dull with disdain,
Widened as colours bloomed,
With every bale, a new refrain,
In that fabric-scented room.
Pashminas soft as a babe's touch,
And stories woven tight,
Held her gaze in a spellbound hush,
For the boredom had taken flight.
"See here," cried the merchants, eager to please,
As they showed her the work of their hand,
"Threads of gold and all colours of the seas
We wove into this Kashida so grand."
The mother haggled, her voice a chant,
As the child watched in glee,
For every word was an artful rant,
A spirited show till the deal was sealed.
At last, bargaining reached its end,
Mother plucked the purchase with pride,
The daughter peered in, with hopes to mend,
Her heart, in the bag's divide.
But there was naught but the shawls within,
No treasure for her to see,
And her heart sank low, with a growing din,
As she turned to her mother's plea.

With a cheeky smile that softened the night,
And her arm reaching in deep,
She pulled out a package, wrapped so tight,
A secret the folds did keep.
Inside lay a pheran, pink as dawn,
With threads of silver spun,
The misery from her face was gone,
With elation she overrun.
So, through Srinagar's streets tonight,
They walked with their treasures dear,
And the child, in her pink pheran bright,
Felt the first joy of Navreh, this year.
For in the market's magical maze,
Where fabric fables found their start,
A happy child skipped on in a joyful daze,
With love embroidered in her heart.

The Shikara's Promise

In the cradle of the morning, the lake lies still,
A mirror to the heavens, where dreams distil.
The paddle dips, like a tender hymn in the air,
As the shikara glides along, like a silent prayer.
I stand beside my father, wrapped in the fold,
Of his pheran's warmth, a sheltering hold.
The cool breeze wakes me from night's soft pull,
As I peer into the sky, serene and full.
The shikara appears, a spectre bright,
Its wooden wings brush the deep.
A lady's call, like morning light,
Her voice stirring, yet I choose to keep

Myself behind my father's frame,
Her flowers bright, her smile aglow,
But shyness holds me, halts my aim,
As her paddles move, and away she goes.
The boat drifts off, the sound of oars depart,
And a quiet sorrow rises in my heart.
I wish for the shikara to return, to stay,
Yet it fades into the bustle of the day.
But then I turn, and lo, a sight—
A single rose amid marigolds fair,
Glistening in the morning's light,
A promise whispered in the air.
For though the shikara drifts away,
Upon this lake where stillness reigns,
I know she'll return another day,
And bring her flowers to me again.
In the stillness of the water, I find my peace,
A gentle reminder that all things cease,
Yet in their passing, they leave behind
A trace of beauty, for the soul to find.

Wanvun Whispers

In the gathering dusk, as shadows sway,
Womanly voices rise, gentle yet firm,
They sing the Wanvun, that ancient play,
As the night rolls by, still and warm.
My sister, radiant in her bridal hue,
Listens, her heart heavy with the weight of change,
The Devagon speaks of all that is new,
Of the paths she'll tread, some merry some strange.
I stand apart, a child in awe,
My world tilts as I watch her go.
The haunting song, so old, so raw,
Speaks of love, and what it means to grow.

But within the beauty of the song,
A sadness creeps, a soft, low hum,
For soon she'll leave, where will I belong?
The home I knew will come undone.
Yet the Wanvun promises a bond,
A thread that ties us, strong and true.
No matter where she goes beyond,
She'll carry with her this sky, this view.
The Wanvun's sweetness will still remain,
A song of love that transcends it all.
As ever I reach out, she'll be there again,
A sister, a friend, my most favourite doll.
And in this home, forever we'll be
Bound by the Wanvun's melody.

The Crimson Veil

Down the winding lanes of this busy, bustling town,
In the shadowed light of day, a mother sought a gown,
The market buzzed with vibrant thread, colours rich and bold,
She searched for cloth of deepest red, the finest ever sold.
"Bring me the best pashmina shawl, with crewel's delicate art,
Show me shades where blossoms fall to warm my daughter's heart."

The shopkeeper smiled, with knowing eyes, and
drew forth silks aglow,
"Here is a saree, where chinars rise, and streams of
saffron flow."
She bartered hard, she traded long, for the best her
love could buy,
She dreamt of her daughter, sweet and strong,
beneath a bridal sky.
But as she reached for the silken fold, a shadow
crossed the day,
A whisper came, a story told, that stole her dreams
away.
For in the valley, dark and deep, where terror's
shadows roared,
Her daughter lay in endless sleep, now all but
blood and gore.
Metal teeth cruelly bit and tore, as the wood saw
split her form,
The bride-to-be could not flee, and was lost to a
monstrous storm.
The market hummed, but hearts grew still, in the
city's bustling lane,
The saree red, once meant to wed, would now
enshroud her frame.
The threads of gold, the colours bright, now bore a
sorrowed sheen,
As tears fell in the evening light, upon the crimson
scene.

And so, she walked, with heavy tread, the saree in
her hand,
To dress her child, now cold and dead, killed over
this war for land.
The market's song, a mournful tune, echoed in her
ears,
As she wrapped her love in the silken cocoon and
bid farewell with tears.

Kongposh's Lament

The dawn dripped down in dew-dappled light,
As the valley stirred to the sun's first sight.
In fields where the earth and heavens meet,
The child wandered on soft, silent feet.
With eyes full of wonder, the little one spied,
The kongposh nestled where shadows hide.
A bloom so bright in the bramble bed,
With petals like whispers, hues of lavender and
red.
The winds whispered secrets, soft and slow,
As the child crept close in the early glow.
Hands so tiny, trembling with delight,
Caressed the treasure in the golden light.

But shadows shifted where the mountains lay,
And hands, unseen, moved to take it all away.
The child stood still, in a daze of dawn,
As the flower was plucked, a bloom withdrawn.
And there from the soil where the kongposh grew,
The child's gloomy hand slowly withdrew.
The flower gone, its fragrance remained,
A ghost of beauty, in sorrow stained.
A symbol of life, both fleeting and fair,
Claimed by time, without a care.
Yet the child remembered the touch of the bloom,
And the beauty that came before the gloom.
For in the fields of Kashmir's past,
The kongposh lived, but it couldn't last.
From flower and the tyok, saffron did fade from sight,
Plucked from the valley, on a fateful night
And so, it still lingers, the kongposh's lament,
A tale of beauty, now remembered just by its scent.

The Bulbul Speaks

Come closer, my fledglings, and hear this mournful
tale,
Of a night when peace was lost, and our dear valley
went pale.
While the breeze hummed and fields swayed in a
saffron dance,
A dark shadow was looming, cruelly awaiting its
chance.
'Twas a night in the winter's cold, January's bitter
breath,
When the valley quaked with fear, and echoed cries
of death.

The winds that once bore songs of joy, now carried
screams so loud,
As fear swept through our homeland, veiled in a
darkened shroud.
In homes where warmth and laughter thrived, a
dreadful silence grew,
For on this night, the skies turned red, and hope
was lost from view.
The woods, once filled with children's play, were
now but empty glades,
As families huddled close and cried, a melancholic
serenade.
As girls were dragged, their honour snatched, the
bloodied earth just wept,
Pandits were spat at, shot or sliced, while men in
power slept.
"Take our oath, praise our lord", was the mob's
decree,
"Or the valley will be cleansed tonight, with your
blood need be."
O fledglings dear, the cries you hear, were once a
joyous song,
But now they tell of neighbours turned, where
trust had gone all wrong.
High mosques, where prayers once arose, now
blared with hateful cries,
Calling forth a night of dread, beneath aghast
skies.

This tale of woe now deaf with screams, of those
orphaned by hate,
Found families fleeing their ancient homes and
swallowed by their fate.
The hearths that warmed the valley folk were cold
by morning's light,
As thousands left with tearful eyes, and hearts
consumed by fright.
The memories of this fateful eve, etched deep in
every heart,
Tell of a time when all was lost, when loved ones
had to part.
The chinars bled, the saffron sighed, the streams
ran slow and cold,
For the valley that once bloomed with life, now
bore a wound untold.
O fledglings dear, let not despair consume your
tender wings,
For even in the darkest night, a hopeful song still
rings.
And though our valley's heart was torn, its spirit
will arise,
For in our memories and dreams, the valley never
dies.

The Man And His Book

I squint into the daylight as the hot earth burns my
feet,
there he is, I believe—sitting by the window seat.
I race up the stairs, the door open wide,
reassured, I step inside, though fiercely trying to
hide
The fear that gnaws, the apprehension
that I might be too late—
that instead of his smile, I might face a closed gate.
I call out gently; a weak nod is all I receive.
I settle on the sill, talking endlessly, trying hard to
retrieve

precious "remember that" moments...But then I
pause—what good would it do?
They say this man can't recall, even if he wanted to.
How could it be? He taught me all I know of life...
He made me ponder, made me think, made me
write.
The mountains and the valley, where our roots lie
deep,
echo in his stories, and in all the memories I keep.
He spoke of saffron fields lush and skies so alive,
He spoke of a land that let many a soul thrive.
With a peck on his cheek and tears brimming,
I wander down the corridor, not caring where it
leads,
When I hear a faint whisper—"Kid, did you bring
anything for me to read?"
With childlike hope, his searching eyes reach out
to me,
I rush back, my heart pounding, clutching that
bundle of sheets.
He takes his book, and in that moment, my doubts
disappear—
There stands the man who once told me stories,
Fables from far and near.
We used to sit together, laughing by the brook...
Now I stand alone, watching as he walks away—the
man with his book.

The Final Return

"Sit beside me, little one, and let me share a story bitter,
Of days when our world turned to ashes, our homes lost in a flitter.
We fled with naught but our memories, leaving behind all we held dear,
To these camps of despair, where each day was marked by suffering and fear.
As we journeyed to this barren land, scorched hearts crying in dismay,
And souls too stunned to speak, of horrors that marked the day.

The sun beat down upon us, unyielding, as fever took its toll,
And the snakes that slithered in the dark claimed more than just one soul.
There was a time, not long ago, when our hearts were full and spry,
When we walked with a straight spine, not cowering and disguised.
But now, my child, we beg for scraps, our dignity stripped bare,
In these dusty lanes of sorrow, where hope is lost to the air.
But listen close, for I have chosen, in my heart, a path anew,
To return to the valley we once called home, where troubles were but a few.
For I'd rather face the end beneath the boughs of my poplar tree,
Than linger here in this endless mire, where life is just misery.
They tell me death awaits me there, in the land of our fathers' birth,
But I prefer that to a thousand deaths I die, each day on this cursed earth.
I'd rather take my chances in the place where my soul can freely breathe,
Than live each day with a broken heart, with naught but sorrow to keep.

So, forgive me my little one, as I take this journey
back,
Remember I go not in fear, but with hope in my
trampled heart.
For even if I meet my maker, near the ruins that
were my home,
At least I'll rest in peace, dear, a worthy end to my
life's tome.
Remember, child, in you resides the fragrance of
our ways,
You are what I leave behind, my cherished legacy
of glory days.
And though this journey ends for me, it is but the
beginning for you,
Carry our stories in your beautiful heart and tell
your children too."

Old Echoes Of Shalimar

Surrounded by the orchard as sunlight weaves,
Through branches wide and tangled leaves,
I wander, a child speaking to trees,
Soaking away in the melodies,
My childhood tales, etched in bark and root,
In every blossom, in every fruit.
The walnut tree, with its arms stretched high,
Grins down at me from the azure sky.
"Remember the day you dared to climb,
And touch the clouds? Oh, what a time!
Your laughter echoed in the breeze,
As you swayed like a sailor on the seas."
The apple tree, with a knowing nod,
Reminds me of days when I was awed

By the fruits it bore, red as the dawn,
And how I feasted until they were gone.
"But beware, young one," it seems to say,
"Too much of a good thing takes its toll one day."
Then there's the cherry tree, old and wise,
With stories hidden in its quiet guise.
"Do you recall the bear who came,
To feast on cherries with no shame?
You watched, wide-eyed, in silent awe,
As he devoured them raw, without a flaw."
The almond tree, with its sturdy frame,
Calls out to me, "You know my name.
It's I who caught you when you fell,
From a stealthy plan that didn't go well.
I held you safe, my branches strong,
As you found your way back to where you belong."
Each tree a friend, a faithful guide,
In this orchard where nostalgia resides.
I played, I laughed, I listened close,
To every whisper, to every boast.
"Come, rest a bit longer," the trees in chorus say,
"Linger in our shade, for another day."
Their voices blend with the stream's soft song,
As I lose myself and just play along.
In this orchard, where past and present meet,
I find my solace, pure and sweet.
I hear the garden's enchanting lore,
And find I'm that young child once more.

O Mother Mine

In the heart of the valley, where rivers meander as they choose,
There blossomed a girl Nimmi, tender as the first snow of winter,
Her frame, petite and delicate, like the petals of a fresh bloom,
Yet within her chest, a heart of iron, a will as strong as the mountain's root.
Born of a land where the sky with reverence, kisses the earth,
She moved with the quiet grace of morning mist,
And although she sways like shy breeze among the trees,
Fiercer than a thousand suns, her resolve took birth.

She, who was but five feet tall, towered in strength
unseen,
Her hands, worn with the labour of love,
Crafted futures from the simplest things,
And in her gaze, we found the wisdom of the ages,
soft yet unyielding.
Mother, the weaver of our dreams, the keeper of
our trust,
You stitched our lives with threads of gold,
Fed our bodies and minds with the food of your
love,
And in the shelter of your arms, we grew strong
and robust.
In the chill of winter, your warmth was our fire,
In the bloom of spring, your laughter, our song,
You, who carried the weight of our world with
grace,
Taught us to stand, to never surrender when life
grew dire.
Your love, boundless as the sky above,
Spilled over into the lives you touched,
A beacon of kindness, a pillar of strength,
Guiding us, even as time etched lines on your
brow.

Oh, Mother, you embody the spirit of Kashmir for
me,
Untamed, undaunted, ever resilient, ever true,
And though we may be far from the valleys that
bore us,
In your lap, we find more than we lost, in you,
paradise we see.
So let this poem be my humble offering small,
A tribute to the strength in your gentle hands,
The courage in your quiet heart,
And the infinite love that makes you, my dearest
Mother, the finest gift of all.

My Orange Bucket

I remember the day we moved in,
A new home, walls freshly spun,
My father's dream, built with love, brick by brick,
He thought it would last us years; it would do the
trick.
Amid the laughter, the bustling feet,
A gift was placed, simple and neat—
An orange bucket with a sturdy lid,
For a girl no more than three, a kid.
How proud I was of that bucket bright,
My one true possession, what a delight!
I'd trot around our new-found space,
Labouring to fill it up, going red in the face.

I'd watch the goats that wandered near,
Feeding them with hands sincere.
Each day was filled with simple joys,
No grandiose demands, no costly toys.
For my parents, this home was grand,
A testament to the toil of hand.
A place where dreams were made to last,
A shelter, from the world so vast.
But then the winds of change did blow,
And with it, fear began to grow.
The exodus called, we were forced to leave,
Our hearts weighed down, with no time to grieve.
In that moment, as we turned away,
I learnt what words can never convey—
That brick and mortar, stone and wood,
Could never mean what family could.
For in the end, as we walked out,
It wasn't the bucket, nor the house,
But the hands that held me tight and near,
That truly mattered, year by year.
My bucket, my home, they were but a part,
Of a larger love that filled my heart.
For though we left, and though we lost,
What truly stayed, came at no cost.
As I look back with tender care,
At that orange bucket, now beyond repair.
A symbol of a time and place,
Where little things held so much grace.

And though that home is now long gone,
The memories of that life live on.
The unending love wrapped in warm embrace
was the best gift our family did ever purchase.

Child In Time

I'm looking for the pebble that shone like the sun,
Search guiltily for the stamped-out anthill, with
probably no ants left... ah huh... none.
I'm looking for the wristwatch I dismantled and
the woven tablecloth that came undone,
Still trying to uncover the place where I hid that
stolen sweet bun.
The time I earned my first bruise as I grazed my
knee,
When I was busy trying to catch that ladybug,
which I did... oh, the glee!
I'm looking for my very first backpack,
And a note from my teacher; she believed it was
obedience I lacked.

I'm searching for that mud puddle which I simply
adored,
It was heaven for me, the place to be when it
poured.
That first toffee wrapper, the sweet that painted
my tongue all the way,
My little bucket when I was the self-appointed
gardener for the day.
The time I ran behind the Tonga till I was
completely out of breath,
The night I cried myself to sleep over the poor
tadpole's death.
The day I ate all by myself, fed my nose too, along
with the rest of my face,
And the time I pranced about in only my
bloomers, but with incomparable grace.
It was a time when my world was just my home
and the garden outside,
Times when "distasteful food thrown away" was
the only reason I lied.
There are millions of things scattered and strewn; I
hope you don't mind it,
You see, I'm trying to gather my childhood. Will
you help me find it?

On Shoulders So High

On shoulders so high, we soared through the light,
Two sisters with laughter shining in our eyes.
In the garden of our home, you were the sun,
Warming our hearts, making life fun.
You carried us both, so steady, so sure,
Even choosing honesty over the obscure.
You'd spin silly stories, never for a moment shy,
Teaching us to question, to reach, to try.
With every word, you'd plant a seed,
Encouraging us to learn, to lead.
We'd argue our points, we'd stand our ground,
With trust in our intent, you never did frown.
Small outings became adventures fine,
You'd capture moments, memories divine.

With your camera in hand, and your girls in tow,
Our laughter peaked; the worldly racket did slow.
And even when they snatched all you had,
You stood tall and stoic; never growing sad.
With indestructible resolve that never did kneel,
You worked hard to provide us a future real.
You too grew with us, as we found our way,
Guiding us gently, day by day.
And when the time came to let us go,
You did so with tears, but your face aglow.
On shoulders so high, you lifted our dreams,
Through the hardest of times, or so it seems.
You showed us strength in the face of loss,
A lesson in love, no matter the cost.
And now, as we walk our own paths wide,
We carry your wisdom and wit as our guide.
And as we walk through time, we finally see,
What a true blessing our life has been.
For on shoulders so high, we reached for the sky,
But it was you, Papa, who first taught us to fly.

The Song Of Sharada

In the shadowed nook of our ancient home,
Where the gurgling stream whispers tales
unknown,
I found an old lady, her hands like the earth,
Worn and weary, yet full of silent mirth.
"Come, little one," she beckoned to me,
"Let me show you the script of your ancestry."
Her voice, like the rustle of autumn's breath,
Carried the weight of life and death.
She unfurled a parchment, yellowed with time,
Where the letters of Sharada began their climb.
"See these marks?" she whispered low,
"They once made the rivers of knowledge flow."

Her fingers traced the lines with care,
As if touching something precious, something rare.
"This script, like me, has seen better days,
But it holds the light of ancient ways."
I gazed at the script, so strange, so old,
Sensing the stories it could unfold.
"It's like you," I said, "worn but wise,
Holding secrets of the earth and skies."
She smiled, a tear in her aged eye,
"Yes, child, like Kashmir, it cannot die.
Though battered by time, and lost to sight,
Sharada still holds its sacred light."
"Will it bloom again?" I asked with hope,
As her fingers tied the fraying rope.
"If you learn its song, if you hold it dear,
Sharada will live, my little seer."
And so, with her voice, both soft and strong,
I learned of a script that carried along
The dreams of my people, the soul of the land,
In the old woman's tale, I began to understand.
That in the script's revival, in the ink's gentle flow,
Lies the promise that the valley's heart would grow.
For if wisdom of Sharada calls us near,
Its beautiful symbols, beckoning clear—
To come forward and heed the silent plea,
Let's immerse ourselves in its ancient sea.

A Valley Rising

When time was young, and earth a verdant sphere,
There bloomed a land, so pure, so lush, so dear.
As this place arose, tranquil waters did glide,
And mountains stood as guardians at its side.
From primal depths, where serpents coiled and
swayed,
Rishi Kashyap awoke, and with his power, laid
A valley bare, where once a lake did sleep,
A cradle of life was born, as silent waters did
recede.
In this fair land, where Shaivism took its root,
Where sages walked, and scholars bore their fruit,

As a beacon of wisdom, this valley did shine,
A jewel where knowledge met the divine.
At Kalhana's hand, the quill moved back and forth,
A land was written, cosily perched in the north.
O' Rajtarangini, you tale so vast,
Of kings and wars, and glories of the past.
Here, in this vale, where streams like crystal run,
And snow-capped peaks do glisten in the sun,
The chinar trees, with leaves of fiery hue,
The saffron fields, where golden dreams accrue,
The people were gentle, as gentle could prove,
Their hearts without malice, their spirits true.
In harmony, they lived, with earth and sky,
And time held its breath, lest things go awry.
O valley, let the ages speak of thee in song,
For in thy beauty, none can ever do wrong.
Kashmir, you're where nature's favours blend,
In thee, the world begins; in thee, the world shall
end.

Glossary

1. **Hameen Asto** (Poem: *Hameen Asto*):

   o **Background**: Taken from the Farsi couplet by Amir Khusrao, in which he speaks of the beauty of Kashmir, "Agar firdaus bar roo-e zameen ast, Hameen ast-o hameen ast-o hameen ast." The lines translate to, "If there is a paradise on earth, it is this, it is this, it is this."

2. **Raghunath Mandir** (Poem: *Hameen Asto*):

   o **Background**: A centuries-old heritage shrine dedicated to Lord Ram, it is one of the most revered temples in the valley; constructed by Maharaja Gulab Singh in 1835 and completed by his son Maharaja Ranbir Singh in 1860.

3. **Tulmul** (Poem: *Hameen Asto*):

   o **Background**: A village in Ganderbal, about twenty-five kms from Srinagar, which houses the temple of Mata Kheer Bhawani (also known as Ksheer Bhawani or Mata Ragnya Devi Temple), a shrine constructed over a freshwater spring and dedicated to a reincarnation of Goddess Durga.

4. **Shankaracharya** (Poem: *Hameen Asto*):

    o   **Background**: Believed to be one of the oldest shrines in the valley, the Shankaracharya temple is situated at an altitude of 1100 ft. above the city of Srinagar, on the Gopadari Hill. Dedicated to Lord Shiva, this temple is named after one of India's greatest philosophers, who visited the valley about ten centuries ago.

5. **Chinar** (Poem: *Hameen Asto, The Crimson Veil, The Bulbul Speaks and A Valley Rising*):

    o   **Background**: A large, majestic tree found in the valley, known for its broad leaves that turn golden-red in autumn. Known for its longevity, Chinar is part of the living heritage of Kashmir.

6. **Hukkus Bukkus** (Poem: *Hukkus Bukkus*):

    o   **Background**: A poem said to be composed by a great mystic and poet Lalleshwari (also known as Lal Ded) about her experience with spirituality; the verse has become a children's song over the years. "Hukus Bukus Telli Wann Che Kus, Onum Batta Lodum Deag, Shaal Kich Kich Waangano, Brahmi Charas Puane Chhokum, Brahmish Batanye Tekhis Tyakha. Itkayne Ne Itkayne, Tse

Kus Be Kus Teli Wan Su Kus, Moh Batuk Logum Deg, Shwas Khich Khich Wang-Mayam, Bhruman Daras Poyun Chokum, Tekis Takya Bane Tyuk." It translates to "Who are you and who am I, then tell us who is he the creator that permeates through both you and I, Each day I feed my senses/body with the food of worldly attachment and material love, For when the breath that I take in reaches the point of complete purification, It feels like my mind is bathing in the water of divine love, Then I know I am like that sandalwood which is pasted for divine fragrance symbolic of universal divinity. I realise that I am, indeed, divine."

7. **Layf** (Poem: *Winter's Embrace*):

    o   **Background**: A traditional Kashmiri blanket with a removable outer cover, typically white or cream in colour, used especially in the chilly winter months across Kashmiri households.

8. **Kangri** (Poem: *Winter's Embrace, The Nocturne of Herath*):

    o   **Background**: A traditional Kashmiri portable fire pot made with hot coals, often carried under traditional woollen robes to keep warm in winter. Kangri is also used as symbolic fire in many ceremonies and rituals.

9. **Herath** (Poem: *The Nocturne of Herath*):

    o **Background**: One of the biggest celebrations for the Kashmiri Pandit community, once elaborate with its week-long preparation and daily prayer. Known as Mahashivratri, this event is dedicated to Lord Shiva and celebrates his divine union with Goddess Parvati.

10. **Zabarwan** (Poem: *The Nocturne of Herath*):

    o **Background**: Situated between the Himalayan range and Pir Panjal, the Zabarwan is a sub-mountain range located in the central part of the valley. Mount Mahadev is the highest peak of this range and happens to be the most elevated part in Srinagar.

11. **Kailash** (Poem: *The Nocturne of Herath*):

    o **Background**: Mount Kailash, a sacred peak in the Himalayas believed to be the abode of Lord Shiva.

12. **Kalash** (Poem: *The Nocturne of Herath*):

   o   **Background**: A sacred metal or earthen pot, often filled with water, flowers, and other offerings in Hindu rituals.

13. **Tchot** (Poem: *The Nocturne of Herath*):

   o   Background: A Kashmiri term for the traditional rice bread, served as prasad during religious occasions like Herath.

14. **Salaam / Herath Kharch** (Poem: *The Nocturne of Herath*):

   o   **Background**: The day following Mahashivratri is also known as Salaam locally. On this day, a form of pocket money, known as Herath Kharch, is given to younger family members as a blessing during the festival.

15. **Pashmina** (Poem: *An Embroidered Tale, The Crimson Veil*):

   o   **Background**: A fine type of wool, known for its warmth and softness, obtained from the Changthangi goat, traditionally used to make luxurious shawls in Kashmir.

16. **Pheran** (Poem: *An Embroidered Tale, The Shikara's Promise*):

    o **Background**: A traditional Kashmiri long, loose gown worn by both men and women, especially during the cold months.

17. **Sozni** (Poem: *An Embroidered Tale*):

    o **Background**: A delicate and intricate form of Kashmiri embroidery, typically done on pashmina shawls or fabrics.

18. **Kashida** (Poem: *An Embroidered Tale*):

    o **Background**: A traditional Kashmiri embroidery style characterized by elaborate floral motifs and symbolic designs.

19. Navreh (Poem: *An Embroidered Tale*):

    o Background: Kashmiri New Year, dedicated to Goddess Sharika, celebrated with special customs and prayers during the first day of Shukla paksha (Bright half) of Chaitra month (March-April) of the Kashmiri Hindu calendar.

20. **Shikara** (Poem: *The Shikara's Promise*):

    o **Background**: Akin to Venetian gondolas, a shikara is a cultural symbol of Kashmir.

A paddle-driven boat made from wood (mainly Deodar trees, due to their water-resistant properties), it was earlier used for the purpose of aquatic vegetation, fishing and transportation. As tourism grew, Shikaras became more elaborate and were converted to floating homes or houseboats, primarily for visitors.

21. **Wanvun** (Poem: *Wanvun Whispers*):

   o   **Background**: A traditional Kashmiri folk song or chorus, often sung during weddings and other celebratory events, primarily by womenfolk.

22. **Devagon** (Poem: *Wanvun Whispers*):

   o   **Background**: A sacred pre-wedding ceremony, it marks the transition of bride and groom from Brahmacharya to Grihastha Ashram (singlehood to family life). This is followed by other matrimonial rituals like presenting the bride with utensils and jewellery, a significant ornament being the *Dejahor* (a gold nugget with tassels strung on a sacred thread to be worn in the ears), which marks the beginning of the bride's matrimonial journey.

23. **Crewel** (Poem: *The Crimson Veil*):

- o **Background**: A traditional form of Kashmiri surface embroidery, typically using long-staple, fine woollen yarn on fabrics.

24. **Kongposh** (Poem: *Kongposh's Lament*):

- o **Background**: The bloom, anthers of which produces Saffron (Crocus sativus), a precious spice harvested in Kashmir, symbolising both beauty and fragility.

25. **Tyok** (Poem: *Kongposh's Lament*):

- o **Background**: Kashmiri word for Tika or Tilak, a mark worn on the forehead by Hindus, at the site of the Ajna Chakra (spiritual or third eye). Depending on the local customs or ritual in question, it is commonly made with Kumkum, Vibhuti, or sandalwood paste, with variation in the shape, size, and colour.

26. **Bulbul** (Poem: *The Bulbul Speaks*):

- o **Background**: Belonging to the family of passerine songbirds, Bulbul is native to Kashmir, often used symbolically in Kashmiri poetry to represent beauty, resilience, or mourning.

27. **Poplar** (Poem: *The Final Return*):

   o   **Background**: One of the fastest-growing
       softwoods of the valley, this deciduous
       tree has both indigenous and imported
       varieties that grow in Kashmir. The
       timber from the tree is low cost and
       therefore used for construction in
       addition to agroforestry.

28. **Sharada** (Poem: *The Song of Sharada*):

   o   **Background**: Widespread from the eighth
       to the twelfth century and derived from
       Brahmi, it was an ancient script used in
       Kashmir; strongly associated with the
       scholarly and spiritual traditions of the
       region. This script also gave rise to its
       descendants Takri and Gurumukhi, which
       were used primarily in Himachal Pradesh
       and Punjab. The Sharada, though an
       important link to the history and culture
       of the entire Western Himalayan region,
       has not been the subject of critical study
       and analyses.

29. **Rishi Kashyap** (Poem: *A Valley Rising*):

   o   **Background**: A distinguished ancient sage
       and one of the Saptarishis (as mentioned
       in the Rigveda), Rishi Kashyap is said to
       have created the Kashmir Valley by

draining the lake which originally stood there. As per Rajtarangini, following this creation, he invited Brahmins to settle in this region, thus marking the beginning of Kashmir's journey to becoming the seat of knowledge and spiritual exchange, attracting scholars and seekers from around the globe.

30. **Shaivism** (Poem: *A Valley Rising*):

   o   **Background**: A school of thought and traditions in Hinduism, which is devoted to reverence of Lord Shiva as the supreme deity. The followers of Shaivism are known as Shaivites and form the second-largest religious community in contemporary India.

31. **Rajtarangini** (Poem: *A Valley Rising*):

   o   **Background**: Meaning "river of kings," it is a historical chronicle written in Sanskrit verse by Kalhana (credited to be one of the first few historians from India) in the twelfth century, detailing the history of Kashmir.